Inevitable Conclusions

MOLLY EMERSON

BookLeaf Publishing

India | USA | UK

Presentation by *BookLeaf Publishing*

Web: www.bookleafpub.com

E-mail: info@bookleafpub.com

ISBN: 9789360942861

First edition 2024

PREFACE

I wish you all the conversations you never expected to have with strangers you never expected to meet, much less with those whose bond you'll share forever.

Collections

Nani has started wandering / in certain fits of
dementia / one minute she sits sipping Diet
Pepsi / next she takes off / in pursuit of herself /
once known / a collector / a cook

Fills a grocery cart / with foreign ingredients /
Pez dispensers / jars of gorgonzola stuffed olives
/ cigarettes / marble eggs / bird seed / a birthday
card for a brother that passed away / ten years
ago

Poppa admitted he was scared / the day that
happened / when he confessed / he lost her / and
this man who served in the Marines / who
hunted wild animals / human and unhuman /
pulled every parking brake / at every hill I
stalled out on / is suddenly just like you / and me

Hold my hand / while I remember / standing
over pots / of simmering red sauce / the scent of
torn basil / sauteed onions / the first time tiny
hands / tightly grasped an index finger / attempt
to place that face / that name / that voice / and
piece back / the stories

Sadness is a Friend, Not a Home

I'm dropping off a carafe of tea
It already has cream and honey
A soft apple cake, still warm

The note reads, Treat Sadness as a Friend,
Not as Home.
Love, me

You will make it through this day
Just as others do every passing moment
 Breathe

As they fold clothes
Pack away dinosaur shaped macaroni noodles
Set the dinner table, minus one

Let's take a sit on the front porch
Listen to it rain
You know what it is

Grief is pernicious, at times
Nearly unmanageable
With tresses that knot and threaten

She can be a bitch
Unsubtle and unrelenting
A reminder at every corner, of what you had
Of what you THOUGHT you had
Stability and Love and Care and a Future, BUT
WHAT THE FUCK IS THIS?!
Sadness turns to rage and abandonment, starts to
swallow you whole and just as you think you're
in and there is no way out of this house with its
shuddering and clamoring and dark walls and
creaking floors, you hate, hate that he said those
things and hate that you trusted them, and hate
that you're here now upset. You turn a corner
there in the window,
it's you, tears streaming. Behind you on the table
is a plastic container
A green thermos and a note that says,

Turn on the hot water,
Run a bath. Soak until your skin flushes pink
And you smell of evening primrose and lilac.

Comb through the knots
With a calm and steady hand,
Put on the softest T-shirt

Here's a slice of cake and your favorite tea
Treat Sadness as Your Friend, not Home
Love, me

Thoughts from 8B Green Street

The sky is ochre, the night silent. I feel like God or the Universe must be in despair tonight, the stars are not shining as bright as they usually are. It's like someone turned the dimmer down.

I'm laying in the snow and still the world is soundless. I close my eyes and decide to make a snow angel, which I know isn't in the rules of this assignment, but they don't explicitly say NOT to make one.

I felt like a child, a sheepish grin found its way from one corner of my mouth to the other before I could tell myself to stop.

Okay, that was a crunch and I live in the boonies so maybe I should go in the house and warm up. "Don't be such a baby" my inner voice starts.

Ah, so that is where She has been hiding. This is me going into the soundless world. Floating in a dark, cold abyss. It's like a voice from the beyond.

Is this my inner She-wolf talking, like the one from that book I started last year...what was it dog'gone it. Note to self: Google that later.

Back to the world: someone must have rekindled their fire because now I can smell pinon.

This is My Song

One of my favorite poems is by Khalil Gibran
When I came across "On Joy and Sorrow"
I must have been in my junior or senior year of
college
It was as if Gibran wrote the melody my heart
had been silently singing

Sorrow carves deeply into the self
as we experience loss,
of a self we think we are
of a self we loved more than ourselves

When we decide the world is an
unjust place to call home and that the
same morality that helps us to make rules,
Does not allow us to enforce them

Even as sorrow hollows us
joy has the ability to fill it out
You simply must be willing
to carry the heavy burden of truth

Return to Sender

As the daffodils in your yard came to spring /
and lime green came to fleck the willow / light
dancing through the leaves / across my eyelids

As a little girl this is what I dreamt of / as a
young woman resigned heavy heartedly / a life
that simply would / never / get to be mine

As I packed away the pieces of my heart / that I
thought allowed me to love / to be loved

As I decided the moment we met / you could be
my future / but then again / my heart was long
gone

As I left to pursue the passions of the mind / I
was stupidly reminded / of how much our lives /
had already begun / to entwine

As we danced away an entire evening / looking
into one another / quickly answering questions
with / but she's / but I'm / leaving / gone

As we spoke / each hug lasting longer than the
last / each of those pieces I thought I had torn /
and sent away / came back

As with each passing week / each walk / each
brush of hands / each morning tea / each buffalo
wing / each song sung / each vacation / I have
come to love you more

Obliged to No One

I was raised by folk
Who thought it right
To sacrifice their needs
For the sanity of others

I was bullied throughout school
For the way my pants
Stopped slightly before my ankles
For being outdated

"If you want to"
"If that works"
"When you're available"
"Sure, next time"

Around and around
It is my duty to be small
To put others first
"No no, whatever you want"

Wait
This is my life too
I am obliged to no one
What do I want?

What I Want

A cappuccino dusted with cinnamon

To share a warm brownie sundae with you

For the bubbles in my bath to not disappear

To pull off the color red

To eat an extra slice of pizza
without feeling poorly

For Ziva and Bunny to be friends

An asparagus patch
and a berry bramble

To make you a dad
of healthy children

To come to town
without having to tell him first

For my parents and grandparents
to pass peacefully in sleep

The ability to balance
a homestead and travel

Control of my work schedule

 I know I need none of these
at the end of the day

Like I said,
it's a list of wants

We all have one

Pinch Me

I told a coworker a story today / that I've never
told anyone else
I think it's the books I'm reading / A Little Life /
and Finding Me
That has me thinking a lot about / shame / lately
Davis' poses the question / "Who are you?"

I told a coworker a story today / that I've never
told anyone else
I think it's the books I'm reading / A Little Life /
and Finding Me
That has me thinking a lot about / shame / lately
Davis' poses the question / "Who are you?"

Last August when I started somatic therapy /
shame was there
Was it shame I carried / or did shame carry me?

In the story I am seven / maybe eight
The kids I go to class with / already bully me
For my pants that hit two inches / above my
ankle
For reasons I don't remember now
Other than simply hate

I can see the exact place / on the playground
We are walking the edge of sidewalk between /
the grass
and sun-dried mulch under the swings
Someone has told a ghost story / and I want so
badly
To fit in / to be special /
So I pinch myself / and say the ghost did it
Immediately someone says they saw me do it
That I am liar / and weird / and they don't want
to play anymore /
With me

From here on out my memories of recess are
spent / not with other kids
On the swing / imagining a life / practicing my
freefall
Eyes closed / pumping my legs / as if I do it
Hard enough / fast enough / often enough
One day I'll just fit in

I will always be the little girl / who took to the
barn
Every Saturday morning to feed the calves / and
dragged along
An Animal Ark / a Nancy Drew / a Harry Potter
To read to the animals / only after chores were
done

They were my only friends / the only place I
belonged
Where I was safe / from the taunting / and
jeering

Eighteen years / that story waited to be told
The shame I felt / from lying / when I knew it
was wrong
Because belonging / felt more important
The shame I've carried / because I felt I wasn't
worth anyone's time
Unless I was gifted / special / unique

Then even as I took the quiet route
Eight years later / I was accused of lying
That I shaved my head / that I lost that weight /
carried around that Clorox
For attention / to feel special / unique
And I had pleaded my parents / begged my
oncologist
To let me start school / at the same time as
everyone else
Because if I started late / I would be made of fun
/ left behind

In my mid-twenties / my ex-boyfriend accused
me of lying
I was devastated / because I did my best to speak
only the truth

But because I was human / embellishments
occurred on occasion
He said I lied / because I changed my mind
In that I chose to rationalize anything / even if I
didn't believe it in my heart
Lying to him / because his truth / wasn't my
truth

If enough people accuse you of lying
The first lie / so that you could belong
The second / they thought the cancer
The third / you believe miracles still happen
You start to carry that shame / of rejection
After you speak anything

At some point I had to start speaking
When you asked / what I was like when I was
younger
For some reason I thought this story / might
scare you
Make you leave / like others before
But others have stayed / learned who I am
That shame has become lighter to bear
Now I pinch myself / and say / "Look!
We're here."

Good People Come in C's

Good people come in C's
Like Chas
And Charissa
And Christian
And CiCi

Whose patience and softness
Helped me learn the biggest lessons
of the last decade:
That friendship cannot exist,
if you are always afraid of betrayal
Every relationship with a human being
contains a multitude of risk
We will inevitably, at some point, disappoint one
another
but the threat of loss will bring us back
I must learn to trust (myself) and the fact
that the world can take a broken thing,
 fill the holes with tenderness, slap some duct
tape on
and rearrangement it into
something beautiful again.

Some Things Never Change

17

I used to write my college papers two nights
before they were due
I'm combing through the rare journal I kept
A document labeled something austere and
confusing
Because the landscape of my mind is desolate
The digging won't even yield to fossils
Ideas from long ago
Stories I kept in a safe

Fool's Errand

everyone you cross paths with
has a lesson to teach you, if only you're open and
willing to learn it

i disagree,

dating you?
that was a fool's errand.

Cahoots

19

What happens between the event and story
The words we are in cahoots with
As we put pencil to paper

Re-member:
to put back together what exists only in
fragments;
arrange into shape, again
and again

Daughter

I hope I get to meet you one day
That you have your daddy's eyes and high cheek
bones,
maybe my curly hair when you turn fifteen

I wonder if you'll be tall and spindly
Good at Math, or better at English
One thing is for sure you'll be
a Dreamer and a Do-er

I hope you have dad twirled around your finger
And I become his second greatest love
You're the only woman I'd ever willingly lose to

I hope you forgive me when I fail
and trust that I am trying
Working out my own knots and imperfections

You are a Miracle to me
One I thought I would never get to have
As I lived out my days as a spinster
Off the coast of Maine

I will be embarrassing at your games and shows
I will make your favorite cake every birthday
I will teach you, hopefully, how to be sad

How to hold it
How to feel it
How to allow yourself to be held
by someone who cares

I hope the world I see
where your dad and I read each night
Turns out to be true and
That your imagination is free to be wild and
curious

I can't promise that if you want to be an artist
You can leave in the house rent-free
Though your dad might be softer on that one

I hope you drag home wild animals
And ask for lots of pets
They always are the best sort of company

I hope that we turn out to be friends
That I don't mess you up
in a way that cannot be fixed

I hope to find out what it means
to love purely
Without an admission of loneliness or lust or
attraction
Just you and me, against the world

The Wise Words of Deconstructed Christians

Life will continue to move on without me and that is incredibly sad, but also the biggest relief of my life.

They probably aren't angry with you. They are probably hoping you aren't somehow upset with them. We are all just doing the best we can and that's enough. Good friends and family will understand that.

Shit happens.

To accept pain as part of life is to welcome the human experience.

To bleed is to live.

Understanding deep genuine joy takes deep grief.

Mistakes will happen so take risks and accept the outcome. Don't be married to it, but accept it.

Growth is not about being happy and making all
the right choices, but having fun with the
process.

Amor fati, bitch.

...And Four To Go

The land surrounding my grandparents'
homestead is made of every shade of green my
mind can imagine. Worn tractor tire tracks lead
the way to pastures where I learned how to drive
stick shift and picked over milkweed leaves
searching for velvet Monarch caterpillars. Rusty
barb wire fences draw out the property line that
we never paid much attention to as children. An
old red barn with a single silo sits in hibernation
now; the last time it held cattle was over five
years ago. Upstairs in the haymow my grandpa
taught me how to box-out girls who outweighed
me by fifty pounds and pump fake before
draining an eight foot jump shot. It is where I
would disappear to play with barn kitties or cry
if I had a particularly bad day at school. My
grandparents' property was just as much my
home and safe haven as my own house was.

It is February now. We are getting ready
to tap the trees for the upcoming maple syrup
season. Grandpa hooks our trusty steed - a Fiat
Hesston bucket tractor - to the wagon containing
the sap tank, drill, metal buckets, spiles, and
hammer. For the Emerson's this is a family
affair. Everything we do on the farm is done as a

team effort. For the next month when Laney, Dan, and I get off the school bus we will set out and collect the sap while my grandpa tends the fire in the sugar shack. Slowly, the water will evaporate out and when the syrup reaches the correct specific gravity we lug it up to the house in an old green Gatorade cooler to be canned. The resultant deep amber liquid is worth more than gold, both in flavor and time spent with Grandpa.

March is muddy and the days stretch as far and wide as the grey skies. Grandpa sits in his old, blue corduroy recliner that smells faintly of diesel and hay. He is holding me in his lap and telling stories while Grammie tends to the stove making goulash. The smell of tomatoes, ground beef, peppers, and onions permeate through the air making my stomach grumble. He whispers in my ear, "Run down to the bedroom and grab a handful of nuts to share. But don't let her hear you. We don't want her thinking we ruined our appetite." I creep off his lap and run softly down to the hallway and return a few seconds later. Grandpa starts telling a story about the time he and some buddies were chased by a momma black bear after they stole a cub. I wish I would have written those stories down.

April showers bring May flowers. My Grammie has such a green thumb, she has her

own perennial business. Daffodils and hyacinths are at the end of their season, yet I wouldn't dare be upset. I stop at my grandparents' house after track practice as a junior in high school and walk over to my favorite flower bed. Ants crawl over balls of peonies, pollinating them. In two weeks the flowers will burst forth into the world showing off shades of ruby, ballerina pink, cream, and fushia. I hear Milo give an excited yelp and know Grandpa is home. He strolls over to me, takes a hold of my shoulder and asks what my goal time for the 400m race is for my meet this weekend. I complain that the coach has found it necessary to even make me run, why can't he understand I just want to jump? After all, that is what I am good at. He shakes his head. "You need to believe in yourself Molly J."
 I start going to baseball games when a local college decides to host a summer league for players looking to develop their skills in the off season. I don't play, but I like going to the games for the socialization aspect and the fresh popcorn. Midway through the season the manager comes up to me and asks if I would like to throw the opening pitch for the Saturday night game. Of course I want to! Being the worry-wart I am, I rush home that night and ask my brother to help me practice. So we do and somehow I have forgotten how to throw a baseball. I

collapse to the grass in anguish and frustration after twenty failed attempts at getting the ball to Dan. My little brother who is an all-star baseball player nonetheless. Tears stream down my face as I sob. Somehow not being able to throw a baseball has morphed into me being a general failure as a human being. (I've always been a bit dramatic.) Grandpa comes home from a long day of haying on the Roly Poly and asks what could possibly be wrong. He hears my laments, goes directly to the cellar, returns with two worn gloves and a handful of baseballs and spends the next two hours reteaching me how to throw a baseball. The coach compliments my throw two nights later.

My Uncle Tim and Aunt Melissa marry in August of 2010. I am a gawky, four-eyed freak of nature dressed in a lavender dress of respectable length. Kids in my class are starting to date and I have a crush on this boy named Cam who doesn't give me the time of day. Stupid hockey players - why isn't bonding over a mutual love of Monk and disdain for corndogs enough? I feel I am destined to be alone for my entire life. I look at how beautiful my Aunt Melissa is in her white dress and am overcome with sadness. After the ceremony Grammie walks out with me to the dock and says she wants to tell me something.

"Your Aunt Melissa looked beautiful huh?"
I nod.
 "Your Grandpa says that one day you'll be even more beautiful."
 I cry.

    September 16th marks my Grandpa's birthday. We are creeping into an Indian summer and soon will start harvesting corn. My mom has a chiropractic clinic and I am supposed to get off the school bus at my grandparents' every Monday, Wednesday, and Friday since mom has work those days. I am six now - a bonafide adult in my eyes. I can dress myself, go out to the barn alone, and make scrambled eggs. But on one particular Wednesday I accidentally went home instead of to my grandparents' and panicked. I was afraid to be home alone. I have a revelation - I saw Grandpa's truck parked so he must be around here somewhere! I pull my mini muck boots on and scurry over to where I hear the most noise. Low and behold there is Grandpa leaning over the silo loader as the wagon churns out fresh corn silage. Without even questioning why I am there he lifts me into the tractor and I spend the remainder of the day with him.

    This is my first time away from home for Halloween. I miss out on picking out a pumpkin and carving it, frosting seven dozen of my Gram's famous frosted sugar cookies, pressing apple cider with my family, and most importantly: the annual haunted hayride. My favorite part is when Grandpa stops at Ghost Pipe, turns the valve, and an eerie low moan escapes the pipe. To this day I don't know where the pipe goes, nor why it makes that sound. I do love to watch how other people react to it, like when church friends make the drive up for the hayride. Perplexed, they ask Grandpa what it is and he never gives them the answer. It is his little secret.

November and December bring the holiday season. Gram is in a tizzy cooking and trying to keep the house clean. This is a whirlwind time for us too; basketball tournaments to attend, the Christmas pinata to make, neighbors to pull out of the ditch after a big snowstorm, Christmas trees to chop down, cattle to get inside. Life is chaotic and moves at 110 miles an hour. My parents host Christmas Eve dinner and then all the family comes up from Virginia a few days later. Grandpa and Gram try to maximize time spent with grandkids they only see once a year, but I never feel any less loved.

It is January and I am writing a letter. I have lived in New Mexico for a year now.

Dear Grandpa,

I know I could never express in words how ardently grateful I am for the love and support you have shown me over the last twenty four years of my life. As I think back to how I got to be in this very moment, I realize I could not have done it with you. One of the most important lessons you have taught me is what it means to selflessly love others. In a world that seems to lack compassion, it flows from you. I wholeheartedly blame you for the fact that I am still single because you (and Dad) are whom I compare everyone against, which I know isn't at all fair. I was only able to mention a handful of the memories you are part of in the paper above, but to write them all down would require a novel. And I imagine you wouldn't be fond of being the spotlight character of a book.

I wonder if you still see the little girl who used to race barefoot up and down the lawn to the chicken coop. I wonder if you still see the little girl who played dentist on Talon. I wonder if you still see the little girl who you taught to eat apple pie and cheddar cheese together. I wonder if you still see the little girl you took to Trowbridge Farm to get grain. I barely remember her, but I wonder if you do.

I am sorry I was a woefully bad basketball player even after all those hours of practice. I am sorry I didn't ask you to write down all those stories you told me as a child. I am sorry we didn't use the fort you built us kids as much as you'd hoped. I am sorry that I don't call home as often as I should. I am sorry I have accepted less than the love I know I deserve from boys who are not worth my time. And I am sorry for not saying 'I love you' more often.

Thank you for teaching me how to call the heifers to supper. Thank you for teaching me how to ease up on my free throws. Thank you for giving me a father who is a real pain in the ass, but only because I am more like him than I would ever admit. Thank you for being patient with me when I couldn't afford myself the same grace. Thank you for teaching me how to drive.

I hope you know that if the day ever comes that some poor sap ever falls for my crazy self, I will be looking for your blessing. The only way the world will get to see me in a white dress with my hair in a chignon saying "I do" is if you are also there to see it.

I don't know how old I am in this memory, but I remember the swing tied up to the branch of the

maple tree to the right of the driveway, closest to
the garage. I'm strapped in and you're saying,
"One for money
    Two for the show
        Three to get ready…"

Dresses

I've started wearing long dresses
and skirts that hit just above my ankle
They hide the scars that litter my legs
like blazing stars and rumpled blankets
Reminders of all that I've broken,
questions that people can no longer ask
As much as they cover
I still have to admit the color and the swirl and
twirl
Have helped to learn to dance again

Unidentified

We first met at the climbing gym
As your purposeful fingers danced around my
injured hand
I thought,
"This is someone I am going to love."

But good things don't always happen in the time
frame we expect them
I was seeing someone else, then you were seeing
her, then her, and I, him
Always we were on the periphery of one
another's life

Then I took off to follow my instinct
One drunken evening we found ourselves out on
that lake
Afterwards, a hug, that I still barely have words
for
But it felt, just like that day I met you

That we were supposed to end up together. That
you were someone meant to have a profound
impact on my life.

The End

I don't imagine another book of poems will
make it into the world
But here is a conversation piece for the future
To say, "Yes, I did the thing."

Here's to hoping I never have to see a work of
my mine on some dusty old Goodwill shelf

But if this one does, hello!